Prophetically Speaking "Must be Is"

Love, Life, Death

Joy Mitchell-Booker

Copyright © 2021 Joy Mitchell-Booker
All rights reserved
First Edition

NEWMAN SPRINGS PUBLISHING
320 Broad Street
Red Bank, NJ 07701

First originally published by Newman Springs Publishing 2021

ISBN 978-1-63692-974-3 (Paperback)
ISBN 978-1-63692-975-0 (Hardcover)
ISBN 978-1-63692-976-7 (Digital)

Printed in the United States of America

Past Publications

1972 Sayre Jr. High School Yearbook (Sooth Sayre)
Philadelphia, PA

1975 West Philadelphia High School Yearbook
(W.P.H.S. Class of 75)
Philadelphia, PA

The Best Loved Poets of 2003
International Library of Poetry
Watermark Press (Ely)

The Best Loved Poets of 2004
International Library of Poetry
Watermark Press (Ely)

The Silent Journey 2004
International Library of Poetry
Watermark Press (Ely)

Colours of the Heart 2004
Noble House Publishers
Poetry Division,
London–Paris–New York

The Best Poems & Poets 2005
International Library of Poetry
Watermark Press (Ely)

The Best Poems & Poets 2007
International Library of Poetry
Watermark Press (Ely)

Centres of Expression 2007
Noble House Publishers
Poetry Division,
New York–London–Paris

Eternal Heartland 2010
Eber & Wein Publishing
Poetry Division
Shrewsbury, PA

To those in my life who've meant the most.
My husband, my beautiful daughters, my grandchildren,
my supportive relatives and friends,
I give to you a part of me!

Peace & Prosperity

Joy Mitchell-Baker
"2021"

Foreword

I can do all things through Christ which strengthens me.
—Philippians 4:13

First giving honor to God who is truly the head of my life.

Thank you, God!

To all those in my past and present life who have added to my psyche, in thoughts, actions, and or deeds which have made me the person I am today, my heartfelt thank you! Because without you, I could not have written this book. This publication is a direct result of my life's adventures and experiences.

The compilation of pieces in this volume reflect the last four decades of sporadic writing. I tried to select pieces from each decade to give the readers a broad view of my style and to note the changes in it over time.

It is my sincerest wish that you, the readers will find something of yourselves in one or more of the selections enclosed.

Contents

Section I: Love 1
    Remembrance 3
    My Husband, My Lover, My Friend 5
    My Man 6
    Words of Love 7
    Love Is the Way 8
    Love 9
    True Love 11
    Blue 12
    Regret 13
    A Mother's Love 14
    The Wonders of Motherhood 15

Section II: Life 17
    Condemnation 19
    Beginning 21
    Synonymous Adjectives of Meaning 22
    Life's Journey 24
    Life 25
    New Life 26
    The Journey of Our Lives 27
    Adolescence to Adulthood 28
    Black Man, Can You See Me Now? 29
    Woman in Repose 31
    Loneliness 32
    The World 33
    Question 34
    Man's World 35

I'll Fly Away 38
A True Woman of God 39
Obama 40
God's Life Plan 42
Longevity 43
Woman 44

Section III: Death 47
Time Wasted 51
Remember Me! 53
Lost to Death 55
Departed 57
Our Loved One 58
Loss 59
Time 60
Touched 61
Bemoaned 62
The Essence of Helen 64

Section IV: Varied Selections 67
Quotes and Clichés 69
Haiku's 70

Section V: Closing Pieces 71
Sonnet 73
Me, Myself, Am I 74

My Favorite Assorted Pieces From Unknown Authors 77
The Woman I Am 79
Charity 81
Days of Birth 82
Literary Influences 83
Us Is Friends 85
What Matters Most? 87
Stand Strong 88
Perception 89
Before You Speak, Please Think 90

Change	91
We the Church	92
Red Bird	93
The Curse of Division	94
The Defense of Pretense	95
The Thing to Do	96
America	97
Privacy	98
Anecdotes	99
Never	100
He That Findeth	101
The Nature of the Beast	102
The Eternal Battle	103
Out from Under	104
Cycle of Life	105
Haiku's	106
Treacherous	107
Me	108
My Husband's Hands	109
Loose	110
Condemnation	111
Black Man, Can You See Me Now?	113
It Is What It Is	115
Natural Beauty	117
Goodbye	118
God Said	119
It Is Written	121
He That Hath an Ear Let Him Hear	123
Haiku's	125
Change	126
Choices	127
It Is What It Is	129
State of the World	131
Arrival	133
Common Idioms, Colloquialisms, and Street Vernacular	134
Wonder	135

I Would	136
Purpose	137
Noise Pollution	138
Rush	139
Alaska	140
Colorful Anecdotes	141
Defamation of Character	142
Libido	144
Promiscuity	145
My Favorite Famous Quotes	146
Sisterhood	148
Time	149
Music	151
Self	152
Money	153
Greed	155
Man from Corinth	157
Healing	159
Highs and Lows	161
Crack and Meth	162
The Evil One	164
Living Death	166
Destruction	167
Decisions	168
Fear	169
Loss	170
I Believe	172
Grande Dame	176
Reflection	177
Irrefutable Love	179
Visions	181
Haiku's	182
Confusion	183
Wench for Sale	184
Family Reunion	185
Glory, Glory, Halleluiah!	186

Flashbacks, Memories, and Dreams	187
Deception	188
Reality, Subconscious, and Heart	189
Relationship	190
Lost and Found	191
Right and Wrong	192
Fruits of the Spirit	193
Nig'gahs	194
7 Cs	195
Impertinence	196
Superstar	197
Secrets	198
The Earth Is the Lord's	199
We	200
Tomorrow	201
Friendship	202
Help	203
Grandma's Prayer	204
Father	205
Grandma's Babies	206
I	207
Giving	208
Suffering	210
Home	211
Happiness	212
Blessings	213
Jesus	214
Inspirational Acronyms	215
Thank You, God	216
Natural Beauty	217
Ten Things to Remember	218
My Sue	219
Adversity	221
Serenity	222
The Unexpected	223
Victorious God	224

Existence	225
Yes and No	226
The Past	227
Generation X	228
Survival	229
Pookie	230
Mama Said	231
Time	232
Grandparenthood	233

SECTION I

Love

Remembrance

Remembrance of a dream
Of thoughts that seem familiar.
The essence of his touch
And sweet, warm, surrender.

A body like sparkling gold,
Lean, hard, and muscular
The face of an ancient God
Fine, structured, bold.

Grasping! At shallow memories
Of thoughts you wish to retain.
Thoughts too quickly fading
Like tear drops in the rain.

Then abruptly! You awaken,
And find yourself alone
With remembrance of a dream
And a chill to the bone!!!

This poem is dedicated to my husband, Mr. William J. Booker, who is truly a source of inspiration and stability for me. Without his encouragement, I would not have had the fortitude to publish my work.

My Husband, My Lover, My Friend

My husband, my lover, my friend

You ease my burden, soothe my pain
Love away my hurt, make me strong again.

You lighten my sorrow, turn tears to laughter.
Lift up my soul, make me whole.

My husband, my lover, my friend

You guide my path, trust in my reason.
Stand by my side, throughout all seasons.

You guard my secrets; stand in the path of danger.
Shield my heart, abide my anger.

My husband, my lover, my friend.
It's you and me until the end!

MY MAN

There's no man…
Like my Man…!

He's all the man
A woman can stand…!

He's all the things a man should be
He's all the things that are good to me.

Loving and kind
Strong yet gentle

The kind of love…that a woman remembers!

Words of Love

This feeling that I have for you
Is more than words can say.
And it grows and grows and grows
More with each passing day.

The pains that I've caused you
Are even harder for me than you.
'Cause I never wanted to hurt you
Believe me darling, it's true.

These words may have little meaning
But it's the way I feel inside.
I hope you can accept it
Without damage to your pride.

My love for you is like a longing
That only you have been able to satisfy
And I'll feel this way toward you
'Til the day my body dies!

Love Is the Way

Love is the way to a warm summer's day
The heart of two lovers sworn to love and obey
Sworn to love and obey
Each lover must show true trust
Sworn to love and obey
Each lover's love should be a must.

Love is the way two hearts show delight
Love is the way to a warm and friendly fight!

LOVE

Love is like honey…sweet to the taste
Love is like money…necessary to the human race.

Love is like rain…refreshing and new
Love is like love…and me loving you.

A special thanks to my dear friend
Debbie from Louisiana.

This one is just for you and your new hubby!

I love you, girl!

True Love

I wondered when my day would come
When love would find me waiting

Not just the man of my dreams
But the man of my r-e-a-l-i-t-y!

I knew, given time, God would find a way
To make up for the long delay

To trust in him, and wait on him
He would ultimately deliver

A man so perfect for my life
I was predestined, to one day, be his wife

The virtue of patience, joy of obedience
All led…to this day of remembrance

To share what is left of the rest of my life
To the man of my reality, my new spouse

The love, trust, and mutual respect
This is a union that will surpass any test

To find a mate of equality
Was worth the wait most definitely

So I stand before you a proud wife
Presenting to you the man of my life!

BLUE

Lonely and blue
With nothing to do

Sad and grave
From the mistakes I've made

Empty inside
Left only with my pride

My lover has gone away
Far from me he will stay

Pride is little comfort
When there is no one to share

Life's simple pleasure
My womanly treasure

Regret

No one knows the pains I bare
The life I lead, the love I share
The feelings that I have deep inside
Are just a covering for my hurting pride
The happiness and love that should be
Is nowhere to be found inside of me?

How do I let my regret be shown?
When I am the cause of my very own!
The depression, guilt, falseness, and lies
Is a protective covering for those by my side?

How can I let my spirit be free?
Without causing pain and sorrow
Where would I be?

I'd be left outside to face my fate
To expose my true feelings, destroy my mate.

To him these feelings do not exist!

A Mother's Love

A mother's love is a treasured jewel
It is like a gift from God
A mother's love is a precious tool
It teaches us to stand tall

A mother's love can never be replaced
It is the source of all our strength
A mother's love is never ending
It covers us with mercy and grace

A mother's love is sincere and true
It guides us through life's maze
A mother's love is an anchor
That roots us for the rest of our days

In times of trouble and distress
We lean on memories past
Of a mother's love and comfort
It soothes our soul to rest

So on this day, my Mother
We salute you and give you praise
For all that you have done for us
From all the children that you've raised!

We love you, Mama!

The Wonders of Motherhood

The joy of birthing a new life
The wonders of watching them grow
The excitement of nurturing
As they develop, learn, and go

The suffering becomes nonexistent
The labor null and void
The past nine months a distant memory
As we tend to the adored

A new life is a precious thing
To be molded, shaped, and directed
Both spiritually and emotionally
A task never to be neglected

To be the guiding force of a life
So new and unsuspecting
To be responsible for their outcome
It's almost overwhelming

But this is the task of motherhood
One we embrace with our whole hearts
We love them, teach them
Then let them go
Knowing we've done our part.

SECTION II

Life

Condemnation

Do not judge me harshly...
for the folly of my youth
It was before I gained understanding,
and acceptance of God's truth

In my youth, I was seeking...
pleasures of the flesh
Without any regard,
to the hazards of that unholy quest

I was laughing, going, doing...
things I should not have done
Oblivious to the consequences
ignorant of the wrongs

Always self-indulgent...
of the things that pleased me most
Never seeking guidance
of the spiritual Holy Ghost

Under the mistaken impression of living...
while my soul was slowly dying
I was having a good time,
while my Father above was crying

I was not alone...
it was a journey many took
We thought we had it going on
prior to reading the Book

Then dawned the revelation…
of the evils of which I partook
The distance seemed too great to cross
my soul would be forsook

But that is a trick of the enemy…
trying to close our eyes to the way
Through guilt, doubt, and confusion,
causing us further delay

My Father said, "Come as you are…
"I will cleanse you and set you free
"You must choose to love me,
Unconditionally!

Your sins are as far from me…
as the East is from the West
Lay your burdens upon my breast,
I will give you rest

So now I rest within his arms…
free from all life's strain
Thanking God for who He is,
and all He's allowed me to obtain

So do not judge me harshly…
for the folly of my youth
It was before I gained
Understanding and acceptance of his truth!

Beginning

We've only just begun to fight for our rights
We've only just begun to really
We've only just begun.

In the beginning, we were quiet and docile
In the beginning, we were pushed and shoved
In the beginning, we knew no better
In the beginning, it was only a letter

Now the letter of proclamation
Is the key to our future and destination
Now we know where we want to be
And it's not at the bottom like it used to be

Now everybody knows that all power is Black
And there's nothing you can do to hold us back!

'Cause we've only just begun!

Synonymous Adjectives of Meaning

Tenderness
    Warmth
        Compassion
            Understanding
                Respect
                    Loyalty
                        Devotion = *Love!*

Bitterness
    Anger
        Resentment
            Frustration
                Jealousy = *Hate!*

Sensations
    Hot
        Wet
            Tingling
                Warmth = *Sex!*

Deterioration
        Fear
                Pain
                        Agony
                                Darkness
                                          Illness = *Death!*

Life's Journey

At the beginning of life's journey
We are young and full of zeal
Allowing the Lord to lead us
Acceptant of his will

We choose a path early on
We follow it as best as we can
Trusting the Lord will guide us
Leaving all things in his hands

It was during a time of days long past
When fellowship was more than a word
We feasted at the showbread table
We were fed by God's Holy Word

We reached out to all around us
Family and friends alike
To bring them into the reality
Of God's enormous might

So when a child of God retires
Having done all that he's been asked to do
He can be at peace with his surroundings
Knowing that he's followed through

So relax and enjoy your leisure times, saints!
You deserve the best always
Knowing God's promises will be fulfilled
That He will keep you for the rest of your days!

LIFE

"What actually is life all about? Trying to survive in this civilized jungle or just waiting to revolve with the world?"

Life is caring for people
who care for you
Life is sharing with people
who share with you
Life is loving people
who love you
Life is living and living happily
Life is love and I love my life.

Life is smiling
when no one is smiling at you
Life is being happy
instead of sad
Life is being cheerful
when everyone else is blue
Life is not giving into defeat but fighting back
Life is love and I love my life.

New Life

We seek to discover more than the now
In hopes it will lead us to awareness somehow
The thought of things different
From which they appear
Will bring "New Life" year after year

The chance to change things from what they were before
A chance to look back through life's closing door
What's done is done…we can go there no more
We can only look forward to what's yet in store

"New Life" is a mind-set
Of what we wish to achieve
A chance to make good
Of desires yet received

Seek not the misnomer
A false trail it leads
"New Life" is living life
In action and deeds

Waste not precious time
Seeking the unknown
Enjoy what's before you
Making each day your own!

The Journey of Our Lives

Unbeknownst were the subtle teachings,
The small prickling of our mind
To explore our consciousness
For the limitless possibilities beyond

Encouraged to reach outside our dreams
Never to fear the unknown
These were the things exposed to us
Little did we know

To sow seeds of hope, love, and encouragement
Around us as we go.
The vastness of our reach
More than we could see
Generated opportunities
For those like you and me

We were given the very best
By the generation before
To achieve a degree of enlightenment
To level the playing floor

Often I recall
The things that might have seemed minute
To become all that I could be
That was the seed I took!

Adolescence to Adulthood

When I was a child
I couldn't begin to understand
All the problems and arguments
Adults had on their hands

The problems of skills, schooling, and crafts
Husbands with no jobs, their names on the draft

As I grew older, I began to understand
To cope and concentrate with the problems on hand

As an adult, I still don't know why
The price of living is oh…so high

So now I'm old weary and gray
And still I don't understand to this very day!

Black Man, Can You See Me Now?

In the bowels of the enemy death trap, we came
Abused, shackled, and chained
Across the rolling sea
To a land unbeknownst and strange

It was I sitting across from you
Can you see me now?

To the selling blocks we were took
Exposed, examined, afraid, and shook

It was I standing next to you
Can you see me now?

It was I who watched them emasculate you
Break your spirit, try to defeat you
Black Man...can you see me *now?*

It is not the shade of my skin
The size of my waist
The length of my hair
That determines my grace

It is the strength in my body
The love in my heart
The will to continue
That sets me apart!

Hurt and disgraced, we were forced to labor
I never lost sight of my soul's Savior!
Black Man…can you see me *now?*

Woman in Repose

Content to be
Proud woman
Beautiful, beautiful!

Awed by inspiration
Spiritual acceptance
Love me!

Perpetuator of existence
Sustain thee
Through me!

Provider of humanity
Follow me!

Giver of self
Share me!

Leader of tomorrow
Trust me!

For... I give to you
All of me!

Loneliness

Loneliness is:

Having no place to go
No one to talk to
Having nothing to do
No one to share

Being alone—isolation

The World

The world as I know it, convoluted and crazed
Gone to hell in a handbasket, morality's a phase

Trying to please the Lord one day, ourselves the next
Feeling tortured and restricted, like living under a hex

Intellectual's dissecting the Word of God
Finding fault and correcting, don't you find that odd?

The Word is plain for all to see
It couldn't be that simple, or could it be?

The Bible spells it out, plain as can be
While we search for loopholes, trying to make it easy

We delude ourselves to make justification
For our acts of immorality and detestation
Then in desperation, we return to God
In hopes that he will forgive, our endless flaws

The world as I see it crazy and lost
So unnecessary, *Jesus* has already paid the cost!

QUESTION

People
Are we so humane?
That we've lost all touch with
Humanity?

Or is humanity so great,
That we've become inhuman?
Inhuman to sensitivity, feelings, love
Or are we just sheltering our needs,
Trying to rob the earth of its humanity?

Man's World

My poem has no title,
But the question is plain to see
Somehow there seems to be no answer
For a person as unimportant as me.

The world is an empire
For man a simple conquest

To show strength, endurance, intelligence
Is merely a simple quest

To obtain strength and power
From a universe so filled to the brim

Should be an easy task
For a man who's filled from within

Filled from within, with the necessities to be great
Filled from within with inner strength, judgment,
personality, and above all compassion!

Compassion to rehabilitate man
In a world so close to disaster

Compassion to utilize the natural resources
Of which man is the master

The knowledge to utilize all things at hand
The wisdom to expand them toward the benefit of man

Now man has the power to create and sustain an empire
But the world today shows lack of
Leadership, responsibility, and desire

And me! All I want to know is why?

These next two pieces are dedicated to:
Her Excellency, the Honorable Archbishop,
Dr. Gracie LaFavor Jackson
Presiding prelate of Fellowship Churches
United Inc., Augusta, Georgia

Bishop, in addition to being my spiritual mother, you have taught me so many other things that mere words fail to express my sincere gratitude and appreciation for what and who you are in my life.

You have taught me wisdom, knowledge, and understanding in the things that matter the most: an unwavering faith and trust in God and a love for all of His creations.

I thank you for being who you are.

Your daughter in Christ!

I'll Fly Away

When this life is over
And troubles are no more
I'll fly away and my spirit man will soar!

The burdens of this fleshly body
Pain will be no more
I'll be headed toward the pearly gates
To heaven's open door

Yes, I'll fly away one day
All hurt will leave me at last
The sufferings, the anguish
Will become a part of my past

I'll be headed toward
My crown of glory
That awaits me on the other side
Where Jesus waits patiently
For me to stand by his side

Yes, I'll fly away one day
When I do not know
My Father in heaven will send for me
And I will gladly go

Knowing this world was temporary
Merely a passing-through
I'll fly away one day
Having done all that I could do.

A True Woman of God

Her designation is in her walk
Her proof of power is in her talk
Her love is shown in her smile
Her presence and purpose show in her style

The work she does for the kingdom alone
To enhance the worship toward the throne
The call was made upon her life
She graciously accepted to be his wife

She has given freely of herself
Time and again she's passed the test
Giving all she has to give
Proving to others that *Jesus* lives

This powerful oracle from the Lord
Before us sits to be adored
Her day of accolades and praises received
To acknowledge the multitude of selfless deeds

So as we can see!

God's woman has made her choice
God's woman hears only his voice
God's woman surrenders to none
For her, only his will be done!

Obama

Once we were offered…forty acres and a mule
Forty years after segregation, now we rule
The price we paid was far too steep
The lynchings, beatings, and don't forget the po-lice…

The battle was fought, sacrifices made
It took some of our forbearer's straight to their grave
But endure they did, stood 'til the end
Confident in the knowledge that we would win!

Discrepancies between thought, action, and deed
Created unsustainable barriers for this nations need!

Martin initially had the "Dream"
Obama saw it "Realized!"
It is now up to us
To incorporate it into our daily lives

To reach a plateau of evenness
We would have to wipe away separatists
To remove the labels of origin
And all just become Americans

To wipe away labels that makes us unequal
And all just become God's people
Even those who don't profess to be saved
Would benefit from the changes made

To present our nation as a united people
With renewed faith and dedication
Would release the promises of God!

Then we could all finally state
Free at last—free at last
Thank God Almighty we're
Free at last!

God's Life Plan

United in a continuous circle
The world of love revolves
Around man, woman, relationship
Around and encasing us all

Tied together by conflict
The source of all life's pain
A never-ending struggle
To reach God's true life plan

As we go around in circles
Striving, not making gain
We forfeit much inheritance
Fighting to maintain

When, if we but surrender
To the Spirit within
It will lead us to our destiny
God's chosen life plan!

Longevity

Wisdom, grace, and maturity
Characteristics longevity brings
These are evident in your demeanor
Mother, you beautiful queen!
The affection which surrounds you
Evidence of your true worth
It flows all around you
Especially from those you birthed.
Dignified, majestic, and stately
Qualities that merely define you
Barely scratch the surface
Of the genuineness your love creates
The humble woman of God that you are
Affects all around you
It soothes the soul, and calms the spirit
It draws people from near and afar
Steadfast, determined, immovable
Qualities I admire the most
Show me that you are truly
A woman filled with the Holy Ghost!
We salute you on this your birthday
We're glad to be a part
Of the celebration of your longevity
This comes straight from the heart!

WOMAN

The woman who raised me
I refer to as mother
The woman who taught me
I refer to as mother
The woman who nurtured me
I refer to as mother
The woman who chastised me
I refer to as mother
The woman who bathed, changed, and fed me
I refer to as mother
The woman who soothed, loved, and cherished me
I refer to as mother
Mother, where would I be without you?
Mother, who would I have become without you?
Your unfailing devotion
Your unyielding belief
Gave me all that I needed
To grow up in peace
So on this day I salute you
For all that you have done
All that you have given up
For my victory to be won
Words fail to express
The debt to you I owe
I only wish to repay you
And lavish you before you go

We take for granted many things
As we learn, strive, and grow
I hope that love is not one of them
An emotion we all must show
To know that you are loved
Is the best gift I can give
I couldn't have made it without you
It's because of you that I live.

SECTION III

Death

For Randi Lee Mitchell

Sunrise–Sunset
April 1965–November 2003

Dedicated to my beloved sister "Candi," who left us long before we were ready to let her go!

This one's for you, baby girl!

Time Wasted

In my youth, I was optimistic, and the world,
It lay wide before me.

I was strong, vivacious, and willing
To taste what the world held for me!

Then, as I began to mature, and life unfolded before me,
Things were not as I'd imagined, or even dared hope they would be.

So I then became conscientious, to what occurred around me
Situations and circumstances, they now seem to affect me.

Dare I involve myself in the madness,
which constantly surrounds me?
Withdraw, retreat, lash out at the injustices that beset me!

In old age, I've become pessimistic at what lies ahead for me
My youth misspent, time to repent, and
hope that the Lord will forgive me

To spend eternity in heaven would be a great reward.
Too bad I waited so long to seek out the Lord!

In memory of my loving aunt:

A special "I love you" from "Big Joy"

Mrs. Mary E. White
July 15, 1935–July 20, 2005

Remember Me!

When the Lord calls us home
Then home we all must go
Leaving loved ones to mourn us
And face the sorrow

But do not mourn long for me
For I am at peace long last
Look toward the happiness
And memories of the past

Remember most, the time we had
The life and love we shared
The joy, the pain, the laughter
And the days that were never sad

Remember me for the life I lived
The kindness that I showed
But remember most, that I loved you all
And will watch over you wherever you go!

Now during this time of suffering
Be strong and fret not long
For I will forever be with you
In your hearts to keep you warm!

A tribute to the late Mr. Larry Bernard Montgomery

April 28, 1957–August 1, 1986

My Beloved

You came, and stole my heart away!

Lost to Death

My love has gone far away
From my reach, he will stay
In my heart, he will lay
Forever near to me.

When death took him away
Many tears I shed
For the loss of my love,
And the future ahead.

A future much dimmed,
Without the presence of him.

A hollowness of soul,
Emptiness of spirit
That can never be filled.

The knowledge that you are now in the arms of God
Keeps my heart, soul, and mind still.

You will never be forgotten
And always dearly loved.

For my daughter, Christina, to her late husband,
and her in-laws for the loss of their son!

A tribute to the late Mr. James "Keith" Edwards Jr.
September 12, 1980–March 20, 2005

Departed

The time we had passed far too fast.
The love we shared was meant to last.

The depth of my love, strength of my passion,
Will have to sustain me in your absence.

Go on I must, the future I trust, will all be left up to God.
He will make a way.
In my heart you will stay, forever a part of me.

So goodbye, my love, rest in peace.
Know that what was yours, forever I will keep!

Always loving you!

Tina

Our Loved One

The loss of a loved one is never easy to bear.
Time loss that was meant to share.

The absence of your presence, the removal of your smile
Life without your laughter will almost seem vile.

It is at times like these that we lean on faith.
Trust in the Lord that you're in a better place.

While we cherish old memories and glories of the past
Our spirit will be uplifted; our love for you will last.

Gone but never forgotten!

Loss

In times of loss and sorrow
We struggle to deal with the mundane things of life
We carry out the necessities
We deal with the toil and strife

We submerge our true emotions
Attempting to complete a task
Evading our hurt and suffering
Choosing instead to wear a mask!

Mourn out…loud…and long!
Relinquishing hurts from the past
In doing so, you'll survive the pain
And free yourself at last

This part of life is never easy
It is a journey we all must take
Preparations for those before us
The arrangements we all must make

As long as you've done all you could do
Free your mind from worry
Honor your loss with dignity
Find your peace within their glory!

TIME

Time does help heal the sorrow of pain
As the "Almighty" said it would do
The presence of each falling rain
Brings back fresh memory of you!

Touched

My life, you graced with yours
Mt spirit untangled, you set free
Wistful thoughts of you pervade
My constant…*memory!*

The moments shared, were fleeting
Precious memories attained, too few…
Death moved your presence from me
Before our time was through…

Continue onward, my journey
Exist, sustain, I'll do…
Never forgetting your presence
A love shared between two!

BEMOANED

Now that the day of reckoning is here
My heart is filled with sorrow
Pain and loss of a love so dear
That words fail to explain

The loss of my love
Source of my strength
Departed and left me hollow

I'll recall the years
Of life well lived
To endure the days that follow

Within my mind, I survive this loss
Within my heart, I bear this cross

To endure God's will, accept his master plan
To know that you will forever live on
In his chosen land!

A special tribute to the late Helen Little Lee

"To my other Mother"
Love always!

Sunrise
September 7th, 1935

Sunset
July 4th, 2010

The Essence of Helen

Time passes far too quickly
Experiences shared too few
Continued life without you
Will somehow seem subdued
The love we shared
Some will never understand.
How important you were to me
The part you played in my life
The way you made me part of the family.
You treated me like a daughter
Even though you had your own
I never felt slighted or even alone.
You took me in, scared and ashamed
Not knowing what the future held
You told me to trust God, and all would be well!
Not many knew how you made me feel
How you lifted me from my sorrow
Embraced me within your bosom of love
Gave me hope for my tomorrow.
Even though distance separated us
You were never far from my heart
You were my inspiration
You encouraged me to go forth.
Your parting will leave an empty space
A void within my heart
But the love you showed while living
From me will never depart.

Even though your body has gone
Your Spirit will remain with me
For you are a part of who I am
And all that I aspire to be!

Always loving you!

SECTION IV

Varied Selections

Quotes and Clichés

Eternal peace sided with eternal love!

Together they fought against bitter hate!

A significant beauty…

With wondrous lust…

Searches for a timeless Passion!

Beyond the realm of reality

Lies the naked subconscious

Open to all suggestions!

Thoughts for today—and

Dreams for tomorrow—a

Wish for yesterday—that's

Long gone and past

Memories of a yester year!

Haiku's

The snow falls neatly

    Shinning in the morning's sun

        Soft petals of life.

            People live in molds

                Life is a vicious circle

                    How will they survive?

People die easily

        They often live very hard

                Is life all that bad?

SECTION V

Closing Pieces

Sonnet

Love, oh love! Where can I find you today?
Do I search in the hall closet for you?
Or do I stay in my room and be blue
Am I looking for you in the wrong way?

Love, oh love! Where can I find you today?
Shall I go down to the ocean and search
Or upon my window sill shall I perch
And look for you out in the misty gray?

The misty gray of the city's street
Or upon the paved highway toward the beach
Is that where I'll find my love today?

Should I go to the market and chance a meet?
Or shall I let our wandering minds reach—
Reach out toward each other in final retreat.

Me, Myself, Am I

I am...

    Yeaaah!

        I am...

            Who Am I...?

                Let's...see...

                    I am happy...

                        I am sad...

                            Often deep...

                                Yeaaah...

                                  That's who I am.

                                    I am me!

Just plain ol' me
The same me I used to be
But sooome how!

    A new me!
    A stronger me!
    A peaceful me!

To me, just myself
　Same ol' self…
But them again…
　Sooomehow…

　　　　A different self!
　　　　An aggressive self…
　　　　A reaaal self…

Yeaaah!
　That's who I am…
　　　　"Me, myself, am I…"

MY FAVORITE ASSORTED PIECES FROM UNKNOWN AUTHORS

The Woman I Am

The woman I am
Hides deep in me
Beneath the woman
I seem to be

She hides away
From the stranger's eye
She is not known
To the passersby

She goes her way
This woman I seem
While the woman I am
Withdraws to dream!

The woman I seem
Goes carelessly
When love goes by
Does not seem to see

But the woman I am
Knows sudden fear
And hides more deeply
When love draws near

For love might look
Closely
Perhaps…and see

Her beneath the woman
I seem to be!

(Author unknown)

Charity

There is so much good in the worst of us
And so much bad in the best of us
That it ill behooves any of us
To find fault with the rest of us!

(Author unknown)

Days of Birth

Monday's child is fair of face
Tuesday's child is full of grace
Wednesday's child is full of woe
Thursday's child has far to go
Friday's child is loving and giving
Saturday's child works for its living

But a child that's born on the Sabbath day
Is fair and wise and good and gay

(Author unknown)

Literary Influences

Authors and poets who have had a strong influence on my writings are Maya Angelou and Nikki Giovanni, just to name a few. There were many others from that time period who were inspirational. But both of these great writers had a profound effect on my style and my desire for wanting to be published.

I first read *I Know Why the Caged Bird Sings* while I was still in high school, and it touched my soul. It was one of the first books I read by a female author, not to mention a Black woman. It opened up a whole new world for me, the world of literature and poetry. As a result, I became an avid reader, couldn't get enough of anything that was written by my people or any other people for that matter. Her riveting tale of her life and what she was exposed to in her early years made me aware for the first time that no one is above another. We all live our lives based on who we are, where we are, and what is going on around us. That no matter your circumstance, you can rise above it.

Now this was in the early '70s, and being inner-city youths growing up in Philadelphia, we were not always exposed to the arts. So when Nikki Giovanni came out with her poem "Ego Tripping," and it was done to music, that was mind-blowing for me. Those phrases which were so perfectly blended to the music were pure poetic genius, and of course we can't leave out Gil Scott-Heron with his "The Revolution Will Not Be Televised" (somewhat radical). These artists, in my opinion, were the precursor to the onset of what we now call rap. They initiated a new sound for the written word to encompass music that was awe-inspiring.

I have, of course, moved on with the times and exposed myself to various genres of literature and music, but the initial introduction is what captivates and inspires us the most.

Still I Rise
By Maya Angelou
(excerpt)

You may write me down in history
With your bitter, twisted lies,
You may trod me in the very dirt
But still, like dust, I'll rise.

Maya Angelou, 1978

Ego Tripping (there may be a reason why)
By Nikki Giovanni
(excerpt)

I gazed on the forest and burned
out the Sahara Desert
with a packet of goat's meat
and a change of clothes
I crossed it in two hours
I am a gazelle so swift
so swift you can't catch me

Nikki Giovanni 1977

Us Is Friends

Memories and secrets
Laughter and tears
What best friends share
Throughout the years

Joy and sorrow
Pain and fear
Things we've survived
Facing our tomorrow

Experience and growth
Family and friends
Sealed our closeness
As we shifted gears

Motherhood and marriage
Responsibilities the same
Distance separated us
Only time remains

The cycle of life consistent
Realities the same
We're all interconnected
On this earthly plane
How much is remembered
As life runs its course
People, places, events

Times of togetherness
Without remorse

An eternal bond of closeness
As we recall memories past
Lives joined together
Friendships that last!

What Matters Most?

What matters most, in these last days in time?
So many issues affecting mankind
How do we determine what to address first?
Which issues affect life and their inherent worth?

People…money…things…beliefs

Each significant in its own right
Which one will help us alleviate our plight?
Which one thing will start us on the path?
To restore mankind to his previous best

Do we return to a simpler time?
Or forge ahead on this technology vine
To pursue the future for what it could be
Return to a past of memory?

What matters most in these last days in time?

STAND STRONG

The people of God are often tested
Through trials and tribulations
Our faith cannot waiver
Our belief must sustain us

Once we get saved, it is in God we must trust
We can no longer live by the world's standards
It is no longer applicable to us.
The word of God is all we need
To survive in life and succeed

To live by the principles quoted in the Word
To stand fast in the light of his marvelous love

Stand strong and see the glory of the Lord
Stand strong and marvel in his might
Stand strong and accept his spirit of love
It is through the Lord that we live, breathe, and have our being.

Perception

We believe, what we perceive, to be true
Is our perception *truth?*
If truth, then whose truth?
Is it based on our intellect?
Our beliefs, or what we think we see?

When we view an incident
It is our personal understanding
That interprets what we see
Based on experiences encountered
Is it how we believe it to be?

No two beliefs are exact and the same
How we filter it is hard to explain
Each man's interpretation
Reveals his own truth
It's all relative, history is the proof!

BEFORE YOU SPEAK, PLEASE THINK

T	=	is it	True?
H	=	is it	Helpful?
I	=	is it	Inspiring?
N	=	is it	Necessary?
K	=	is it	Kind?

(Author unknown)

Change

Change, like the Earth, is in perpetual motion
Change is also a living phenomenon
You can't stop change
You can't control change
We can only hope to direct the change
Direct it in the way you want it to go
Manage how and when we change

Change is strange
It happens with or without our consent
Sometimes we see it coming
Others, we don't
We simply recognize that change occurred.

Change is the only constant in life.

We the Church

The collective voice of the church
Has been silent for far too long
We've neglected our commission
To help keep our nation strong
Our collective voice has been silent
When we should've been shouting out loud?
We have been quietly asking
When we should have been demanding
It is up to us to lend a guiding hand
To assist those in power positions, help them take a stand
Our light is no longer shinning bright
Our salt has all but lost its flavor
It's no wonder the world is lost
We've not glorified our Savior
We should be the moral compass; we speak out God's word
Regardless of the consequences, in spite of what we've heard
We will be held accountable for not taking a stand
Allowing the world to dictate to us, when we know they don't understand
The Word of God is final, no further discussion needed
Our nation was built on this foundation
Why has the church conceded?

Red Bird

Red bird, red bird perched high in the tree
What does your vantage allow you to see?

Red bird, red bird soaring through the sky
Free and unencumbered, you do fly

Red bird, red bird, how I envy your flight
I wish it was I, with all my might

Red bird, red bird, you never tarry long
From limb to limb, you flitter along

Red bird, red bird, is this the secret of life
To sail along without contention or strife

Red bird, red bird, what a privilege it must be
To be born a creature without responsibility.

The Curse of Division

Why we find it necessary to separate ourselves
In opposing extremes, we divide ourselves

Black against white, rich against poor, young against old
Who is keeping score?

Weak against strong, smart against dumb, haves against have-nots
Where did we go wrong?

Religion against religion, nation against nation,
Shouldn't we all be equal in station?

Where is the benefit for mankind?
If we continue to antagonize and undermine

We'll not only destroy ourselves, but the Earth as well
"The earth is the Lord's and the fullness thereof."

The Defense of Pretense

A mechanism we employ
While trying to destroy
What others perceive
To be the essence of me
We pretend to be this
We pretend to be that
To defend our true character
Or hide it at best.

The defense of pretense is widely used
It's almost become an inherent tool
We wear a mask, disguise our flaws
Trying to appear perfect
This is against nature's law

Why we wish to be other than we are
Is beyond reason, totally bizarre
Be the best that you can be
True to yourself for eternity.

The Thing to Do

"It seemed like the thing to do at the time"
We've all done things we are not proud of
We've all made decisions that we wish we hadn't
But it seemed like the thing to do at the time

We've all gone places that weren't quite right
Said things which may have caused a fight
Looked at a situation, sized it up wrong
When we should've minded our own business all along
But it seemed like the thing to do at the time

Told falsehoods that affected other's lives
Insinuated our opinion, not sure that was wise
But it seemed like the thing to do at the time

Sold our souls, for what we thought was fun
Only to find, there's nothing new under the sun
But it seemed like the thing to do at the time

In life, we all go through a learning process
Making decisions, as we think best
Because at the time, it seemed like the right thing to do!

America

Don't be mistaken
Don't be misled
This is not about you
But the whole country instead
If we end hypocrisy, and stop the lies
We might be able to restore fellowship
With our foreign allies
We're falling fast
We're losing favor
Disliked even by our closest neighbor
Once a shining star
Revered by those near and far
Once quoted the place to be
Offering equality, and a chance to be free,
Where did we go wrong?
When did the tide turn?
Was it sticking our nose where it didn't belong?
Is that what sent us spiraling fast?
Causing others to want to destroy our ass!

PRIVACY

Deceitful illusion
False belief
No such animal
P-R-I-V-A-C-Y

Once upon a time
Technology since removed
Personal information sheltered
Then social media conceived

The facade of privacy
An allusion of the past
All secrets revealed
To anyone who asks

To uncover a hidden
You need only be equipped
With the proper electronics
And a knowledge of where to click!

Anecdotes

When you are stuck between a rock and hard place
Choose the hard place
Because a hard place may soften
But a rock is a rock is a rock.

The truth is the Light
And the Light must shine!

If my eyes didn't see it
My ears didn't hear it
Then my lips shouldn't speak it!

The most important things in life are invisible
Love, Hope, Faith, Belief!

Never

Never say never, for the future is yet unknown
Each day is a new adventure
Circumstances yet shown

We react to the present situation
Never knowing what it will be
To say I will never
Is bordering on perjury

Life has many twists and turns
Which way it will go is hard to discern
What we think we want
Is seldom what we get

Only God knows best
How we will endure each test
So beware of saying never
You just never know

What you may do
To survive in this life
And make it through!

He That Findeth

When a man of God chooses a godly wife
Their futures are intertwined for the rest of their lives
The Holy Spirit will guide their path
To sustain a love that's sure to last

Though trials may come
Your love will stay true
The power of God will see you through

Enjoy your day, you're on your way
To what God has designed for all mankind
To share of yourself, give each other your best
Of what God intended, when he created man in his image

May your union see you through 'til the end of your days
Just put God first in all your ways
His word is true and his love is divine
For I am now yours and you are now mine!

The Nature of the Beast

The nature of the beast is war
For eons, what have we been fighting for?
Some fight for power, some wealth, some land
Some fight for love, some to take a stand

To stand against tyranny
To stand against injustice
To stand against any unfairness toward his fellow man
To determine who's right or who's wrong
Depends on where you stand

The nature of the beast is ever-changing
From the beginning of time to date
War is part of civilization
For man it is innate.

The Eternal Battle

The eternal battle between mind and body
The body revolts, attempts a coup

The mind has to bring it under subjection
There can only be one command center

The power of the mind must control the body
If not, the body will run rampant

The spirit is willing but the flesh is weak
We must renew our minds daily

To control the beast!

Out from Under

To come out from under, whatever your complaint
To go through your trouble, survive and not faint

Never knowing how you did it, just one day it's gone
You look back and wonder, how did I get along?

Perseverance and patience, saw you through 'til the end
Faith and belief, ensured you'd win

Never succumb to adversity, for this too shall pass
Keep looking to the future, difficulty won't last

On the other side of through, you're stronger than before
Never having to experience that pain anymore

A new situation will arise, to occupy your mind
Each day, a new adventure for mankind

This is life's process, a new dilemma each day
It keeps us forever striving, searching for a better way

So come out from under, you were never alone
Because there is nothing new under the sun!

Cycle of Life

Beginnings and endings are the cycle of life
A new adventure begins an old experience ends
We plod along, facing each new day
Striving to make gain without delay

For every life that begins, another will end
Thus the balance in the earth is maintained
All living things must undergo this cycle

People, animals, and even plant life have a cycle
As do hopes, dreams, and aspirations
Accepting the inevitable
Prolongs sanity!

Haiku's

To be a steward
Of the most-high God requires
Generosity!

The wealth of the Lord
Belongs to his disciples
To dispense with love!

There is a direct
Correlation between faith
And giving in Christ!

Why are we afraid
To share with one another
There's no lack in trust!

Treacherous

Be careful whom you trust
True friendship is a must
Make sure you know them inside out
About your friends, there can be no doubt
You cannot judge a book by its cover
Fidelity and loyalty are rare, you'll discover

There's usually one traitor in your midst
Hiding behind a kind word and a kiss
Always there to offer support
Seeking to destroy in a secret tryst

How to protect yourself from the enemy within
Who will it be among your so-called friends?
When will the traitor show their true colors?
When you least expect it
Not a minute further.

ME

Kindness and concern show forth in my smile
Poise and wisdom reflected in my style
The perfection and structure of my face
Show forth God's manifold grace

Determination and fortitude of my will
Promote peace within when I am still
I give of myself 'til there's nothing more to give
Reflecting the love of God is how I live

Day after day, I go my way
Leaning on God as I pray
Portraying to all who see me pass
My contentment in life at long last

The will of God always prevails
When you choose to follow in his trail
Joy and contentment in life are free
When you live in God's liberty!

My Husband's Hands

Strength and character in appearance
Twice the size of my own
Soothe me when I am weary
Gently massage my bones

Repair broken objects
All things his hands can fix
My husband's hands are magic
They never miss a trick

His hands to me are perfect
I have them memorized
For me they encompass
A world in which I thrive.

Loose

Freedom unrestrained
Remove me from me my chains
Released from my misery
Allow God's Son to shine in me

Set loose in a world
One I do not know
Stranger than it was before
Assimilate, acclimate, myself into this place

Support from family
Loved ones and friends
Eased me into this world
Headed toward its end

Time removed does wondrous things
Allows you to appreciate what each day brings.

CONDEMNATION

Do not judge me harshly…
for the folly of my youth
It was before I gained understanding,
and acceptance of God's truth

In my youth, I was seeking…
pleasures of the flesh
Without any regard,
to the hazards of that unholy quest

I was laughing, going, doing…
things I should not have done
Oblivious to the consequences
ignorant of the wrongs

Always self-indulgent…
of the things which pleased me most
Never seeking guidance
of the spiritual Holy Ghost

Under the mistaken impression of living…
while my soul was slowly dying
I was having a good time,
while my Father above was crying

I was not alone…
It was a journey many took
We thought we had it going on
prior to reading the Book

Then dawned the revelation...
of the evils of which I partook
The distance seemed too great to cross
my soul would be forsook

But that is a trick of the enemy...
trying to close our eyes to the way
Through guilt, doubt, and confusion
causing us further delay

My Father said, "Come as you are...
"I will cleanse you and set you free
"You must choose to love me,
"*Unconditionally!*"

Your sins are as far from me...
as the East is from the West
Lay your burdens upon my breast
I will give you rest

So now I rest within his arms...
free from all life's strain
Thanking God for who he is,
and all he's allowed me to obtain

So do not judge me harshly...
for the folly of my youth
It was before I gained
Understanding and acceptance of his truth!

Reprinted from *Inside My Soul*
(February 2011)

Black Man, Can You See Me Now?

In the bowels of the enemy death trap, we came
Abused, shackled, and chained
Across the rolling seas
To a land unbeknownst and strange

It was I sitting across from you
Can you see me now?

To the selling blocks we were took
Exposed, examined, afraid, and shook

It was I standing next to you
Can you see me now?

It was I who watched them emasculate you
Break your spirit, try to defeat you
Black man…can you see me now?

It is not the shade of my skin
The size of my waist
The length of my hair
That determines my grace

It is the strength in my body
The love in my heart
The will to continue
That sets me apart!

Hurt and disgraced, we were forced to labor
I never lost sight of my soul's Savior!
Black man...can you see me *now?*

Reprinted from *Inside My Soul*
(February 2011)

It Is What It Is

Gone are the days of old
Where morality is but a mere dream
No one values life anymore
Or so…it would seem!

Greed and self-survival
Appear to be the norm
No longer concern for one another
Just anger, malice, and scorn!

When did this change take place?
Did it slip in unnoticed?
Were we so involved in technology
That we lost sight of our responsibility?

What's going to happen to our future
When people no longer care for one another?
What kind of example are we setting?
No more brother keeping brother

There once was a time not so long ago
When people helped one another
We took pride in our community
It exemplified unity

The children were taught to care
They learned to coexist
Through sharing

Now what it is…is it's all about me
What will I get from it?
How will it benefit me?
Is this the way to sustain the family?

These questions appear mundane
But the answers will enable us to sustain
What the rest of our future will be
As a people for all eternity.

If we don't adjust our disposition
We may find ourselves in an awkward position
Facing borderline extinction
As a result of negligent intentions

Disregard for one another
No longer brother helping brother
This is not the way
God meant for it to end

It's up to us to end the violence
Where is the love, is it gone away?
It is what it is…what more can I say?

Reprinted from *Lip Service*
(October 2012)

Natural Beauty

Mountains majestic, peaks pointing skyward
A stunning example of perfect creation

Spectacular waterfalls, lush green terrain
Visual imagery beyond acclaim

Sunrise and sunsets, that take your breath away
The artistry of God, impossible to duplicate

Try as we might, all the greats
They do a good job, but only imitate

No one can touch, the Master's flair
Original creations, nothing else can compare

The sky, the moon, stars that shine at night
Only increase our visual appetite

Beauty so pure, it pierces the heart
God's divine tapestry, the world in itself…*art!*

Reprinted from *Inside My Soul*
(July 2015)

Goodbye

Please don't weep for me
Now at last I am free
My earthly pains are no more
I am headed toward heaven's door

I know that you will miss me
I will miss you too
Mourn not long, but for a short while
Then let go of the memory

Just smile and reflect
On times of joy shared
Know I am in a better place
In God's perfect care

So goodbye, my lovelies
Though our time seemed short
It was more than enough
For us to touch each other's heart.

God Said

If my people which are called by my name, shall humble themselves, and pray, and seek my face, and turn away from their wicked ways; then will I hear from heaven, and will forgive their sin, and will heal their land.
—2 Chronicles 7:14

The way has been made
All we need to do is adhere.
Give no credence to the enemy,
God's word is sincere!

Ye are the salt of the earth: Ye are the light of the world.
—Matthew 5:13, 14

We are the seasoning that flavors the earth
Our ways should be emulated for all they are worth.
We should not be led by fleshly desire
Try all things by God's holy fire!

Let not your heart be troubled: And I go and prepare a place for you, I will come again, and receive you unto myself; that where I am, there you may be also.
—John 14:1–3

Have no worries for today's woe
For I am with you wherever you go.
A place has been made for those who believe
Unto myself…you, I will receive.

For God so loved the world, that he gave His only begotten
Son, that whosoever believeth in him should not perish,
but have everlasting life.

—John 3:16

Where is the Love, which was so freely given
To all mankind, for eternal living?
We've turned our backs on God above,
Refused acceptance of his precious blood.
Blood shed for you and for me
To live in love perpetually.
Where is the love?
Where is the love?
Where…is…the…love?

It Is Written

The fear of the Lord is the beginning of knowledge:
but fools despise wisdom and instruction.
—Proverbs 1:7

What we think we know
When we know nothing at all
If we do not first
Recognize, and accept his call.
He is first, before all things
Great success, which only faith brings.
God's desire is that none should perish
It is up to us to choose him to cherish.
To live a life, holy, and acceptable to God
Is not that difficult,
Not difficult at all!
We make it harder than it needs to be
Because we want life to be easy.

We want to reap the rewards
Without paying the cost,
Then be mad at God
When we find ourselves lost!
O' foolish fool, why torment yourself?
Submit to the truth, and free yourself.

What we think we know
When we know nothing at all
Is without right relationship

We'll never stand, just fall.
Yield, surrender, and submit to his word
It is there to teach, and undergird.

HE THAT HATH AN EAR LET HIM HEAR

He, who has an ear, let him hear what the Spirit
says to the churches
—Revelations 3:6

We are born; we live, and then die
It's the way we live, that determines the why?
To live a life which is pleasing to God
Understanding who we are,
Standing against all odds.

God speaks into the atmosphere,
It is for all who have a listening ear.
His instructions are given freely
To those who recognize his voice.

His revelation for us
To be interpreted as we perceive,
Then spread among
His numerous seed.

His message is the same
For all who hear,
Then distributed to those
Who have an ear to hear.

Our spirits should be in tune
To recognize our master's voice,

It's readily available to
Those of us who've made the choice.

He that have an ear to hear,
Let him hear
What thus saith the *Lord!*

Haiku's

The wonders of life
The joys tomorrow will bring.
How gracious is God?

Moisture of dewdrops
Refreshing rain falls anew.
Purity of life!

Time passes quickly,
How will we complete all things?
Life is fraught with rush.

CHANGE

The winds of change ride a slow horse,
The strength of nature an immutable force.
The process of nature can never be overturned,
The inevitability of change a slow burn!

Choices

Quotes taken from the good book,
Many turned into clichés.
What we should've been doing
Is living them day by day.

Everyone wants to live the good life,
Never have we heard it the other way.
How we live is up to us,
Choices we make each day.

We've heard it said, "You reap what you sow"
How it returns, we'll never know.
Give your best at every occasion,
Trust in God for revelation.

The choices we decide
Determine the direction of the tide,
The course of our existence,
The evolution of our future.

Freedom of choice
Is a major force.
It affects all that we do,
Enables dreams to come true.

It is up to each of us
To make the correct choice;

To succeed in life,
Or...live a life of strife!
What's your choice?

It Is What It Is

Gone are the days of old
Where morality is but a mere dream.
No one values life anymore
Or so…it would seem!
Greed and self-survival
Appear to be the norm,
No longer concern for one another,
Just anger, malice, and scorn!
When did this change take place?
Did it slip in unnoticed?
Were we so involved in new technology,
That we lost sight of our responsibility?
What's gonna happen to our future?
When people no longer care for one another
What kind of example are we setting?
No more brother keeping brother.
There once was a time not so long ago
When people helped one another.
We took pride in our community,
It exemplified unity.
The children were taught caring,
They learned to coexist
Through sharing.
Now what it is…is, it's all about me!
What will I get from it?
How will it benefit me?
Is this the way, to sustain the family?
These questions appear mundane,
But the answers will enable us to sustain.

What the rest of our future will be
As a people for all eternity!
If we don't adjust our disposition
We may find ourselves in an awkward position,
Facing borderline extinction
As a result of negligent intentions,
Disregard for one another,
No longer brother helping brother.
This is not the way, God meant for it to end.
It's up to us to end the violence.
Where is the love?
Is it gone away?
It is what it is…
What more can I say?

STATE OF THE WORLD

In a world filled with turmoil
Where will it end?
Life so consumed with achieving,
No time to cultivate friends.
We're losing the art of socialization,
Becoming our own best friend,
No time for one another.
Where will it end?

What will happen to the children,
If we don't change our outlook?
Return to a more pleasant pastime
Of fables, make-believe, and storybooks.
This fascination with violence
It permeates our surroundings,
Fills us from within.
Where will it end?

All of our entertainment,
TV, games, and music
Is filled with violence and anger,
Creating an atmosphere of danger.
It is teaching the wrong message,
The value of life diminished.
It's become a game of excitement
Without regard to the finish.
Where will it end?

If we are to survive the decades to come
We must change the information given
To our little ones.
They look to us for direction,
The way in which they should go.
We are currently promulgating destruction,
It will be all that they will know.
Where will it end?

Will we be able to reverse this trend?
The movement should start now
To capture the next generation,
Turn it around somehow.
Show more love and compassion
For the world in which we live.
This is not the total answer,
Only a place to begin.
If we are not careful,
Where will it end?

Arrival

Naked and alone I came into the world,
Alone I shall probably leave;
The things acquired in the between time
Is nothing more than what it seems?
Most lives are spent acquiring material wealth
Instead of memories,
Something that will last eternally.

What a waste of effort
On useless gatherings,
Things that have no meaning.
We scrape and scruff
Trying to keep up
With what we falsely perceive.

Naked and alone I came into the world
Alone I shall probably leave;
With fond memories of family, love, and God.
What a fulfilling life indeed.

Common Idioms, Colloquialisms, and Street Vernacular

Man up!
Put on your big girl panties!
Suck it up!
It is what it is!
Make it do what it do!

Tru dat...!
Cum...own somebody...!
Dat's...what's up!
Whatz...up!
Well...alrighdy den...!
U betta ask sum...bidy...!
Don't git it twisted...!

Show me what you working with!
Ain't noe kin to me!
It's all good!
Keeping it real!

Wonder

Do you ever ponder
Over other people's thoughts?
Why some do the things they do,
What causes them to be distraught?

I often wonder about passersby,
What their life is like.
It's a momentary awareness
Of others outside my life.

Are they happy, sad, in love?
What does their life entail?
It's hard to determine visually.
Appearances say, all is well.

Things are seldom how they appear,
We never know what others fear.
It just makes me wonder
If catastrophe is near.

At any rate, it's a passing thought,
A curiosity which amounts to naught.

I Would

I would that we could be,
More in control and less emotional.

I would that we could be,
More proactive than reactive.

I would that we could be,
More thankful and less revengeful.

I would that we could be,
More loving and less judgmental.

I would that we could be,
More generous and less self-involved.

I would that we could be,
More caring about people than things.

I would that we could be,
All that mankind could aspire to be,
To sustain the planet eternally.

Purpose

Eternal peace, sided eternal love
Together they fought against bitter hate.
The heavens roared, the earth shook
Reinforcing to mankind, always to look.
Look toward heaven for all reward,
The gift of life, not to be ignored.
Man's existence more than whimsy,
Glorification of God is nothing flimsy.
Our single task after creation
Was to offer to God adoration!

We were created to glorify the master,
To be his companions, before the disaster.
Once defiled, we lost much ground,
Had to wait for *Jesus* to turn things around.
His journey to earth made a way
For us to rejoin the master without delay.
We need only repent and then pray.
Ask the Lord to come into our life.
Live holy, and choose to live right.

NOISE POLLUTION

Sirens blaring,
Motorcycles gunning,
Children playing in the street,
Music out of control,
Base beyond belief.
No one wants to hear that crap,
It only causes us grief!

Cell phone conversations
Everywhere you go,
Profanity ungodly
How were we to know?

How do we remedy
This unpleasant situation?
Restore our solitude,
Eliminate this hullabaloo!

Noise, noise, noise,
Every which way you look.
I want my solitude back,
Who do I have to execute?

Rush

Rush, rush, rush…what's the fuss?
In a hurry going nowhere fast,
Trying to complete things that will never last.

Running around like chickens with our heads cut off.
Scurrying about like ants,
For no apparent cause.

The things in this life are temporal,
They only last for a while.
Let's do things eternal,
Cause our God to smile!

All this busy nonsense
Running to and fro,
Is wasted effort on our part,
All earthly things will go.

Spend less time rushing,
More time on love;
It is the great commandment,
From God the Father above.

Alaska

Crisp, clean, and pristine,
Air pure and sweet,
Cold, invigorating;
What else can compete?
Mountains majestic,
Rivers and lakes galore,
Scenery so breathtaking;
God so awesome
Who could ignore?
The last virgin wilderness
Undefiled or spoiled.
That great expanse of northland
Yet to be explored.
A world unto itself,
The people there unique.
A land shrouded by distance
Still maintains its mystique.
Visit if you can,
Come, explore the unknown.
The last vestige of nature
For man to conquer alone.

Colorful Anecdotes

Too bad, so sad
Not my problem!
(Janet, Arkansas)

> Money don't make me
> I make money!
> (Butch, Pennsylvania)

> Must be is or it
> Must be ain't!
> (Ms. Lil, Pennsylvania)

Snitches end
up in ditches
Requiring multiple
stitches!
(Tiff, Pennsylvania)

> The truth is the light
> And the light must shine!
> (Joy, Georgia)

> What's—n-never!
> (Helen, Pennsylvania)

Yes indeedy, sweetie!
(Butch, Pennsylvania)

> A lie don't care
> Who tell it!
> (Bill, Georgia)

DEFAMATION OF CHARACTER

We have destroyed the integrity of the word
Love
Commonality of usage…
Turned it into a four-letter word.

Love requires a give and take,
You can't love it…if it's inanimate.
You like what you like,
But that's not love.

Love is a deep emotion
Tied to the heart.
Not a plaything
To be used without thought.

You admire a thing, appreciate its beauty.
Lust after the flesh, chase the booty!
People have style, poise, and grace.
To say you love it
Shows a lack of taste.

We must stop defacing the word *love*,
Find alternatives for what we feel,
Increase our vocabularies to express proper appeal,
Show love for things that live.

Where is the charity, the depth of emotion,
The outward results of what we feel?

Love is an action word,
It requires effort on our part.
Not just something to say,
When it touches the heart.

Expressions of love
Are found in your deeds.
The actions you take,
The decisions you make.

Love is love…tried and true.
It's not what you say,
But what you do!

Libido

Body against body
Limbs entwined
So exciting
Pleasures of the mind.

Joining together
Passions sublime
Sharing two souls
Love's divine.

Flesh against flesh
Heart to heart
Where did it go?
Why did it depart?

Emotions the same
Desire has waned
Time elapsed
Physical pleasure's past.

Promiscuity

Lust of the flesh
Mentality delinquent
Trying to fill voids
Which leave our souls empty.
Seeking love, in all the wrong places,
Multiple encounters, leaving abstract faces.
No depth of emotion, achieved
Emptiness, heartache, often deceived.

Why this torture?
What promotes this need?
Something lacking inside
Which causes this disease.
The desire to feel loved
Often missing from home.
A need not fulfilled
That causes us to feel alone.
Frequent fornication
No emotions attached,
Leads to promiscuity
And feeling detached.

My Favorite Famous Quotes

"There are no facts, only interpretations."

"For every man there exists a bait which he cannot resist swallowing."

—Friedrich Nietzsche

*****

"The fewer the words the better the prayer."

"I have to hurry all day to get time to pray."

—Martin Luther King Jr.

*****

"Too often we…enjoy the comfort of opinion without the discomfort of thought."

"Those who make peaceful revolution impossible will make violent revolution inevitable."

—John F. Kennedy

*****

"Anger dwells only in the bosom of fools."

"Only a life lived for others is a life worthwhile."

—Albert Einstein

*****

"Don't confuse fame with success. Madonna is one; Helen Keller is the other."

"Dreams have only one owner at a time, that's why dreamers are lonely."

—Irma Bombeck

*****

"The price of greatness is responsibility."

"Success is the ability to go from one failure to another with no loss of enthusiasm."

—Winston Churchill

*****

"What lies behind us and what lies before us are tiny matters compared to what lies within us."

—Ralph Waldo Emerson

Sisterhood

More than just a bloodline,
Closer to experiences shared.
Outside race or nationality
Are forged the bonds of sisterhood.

Worldwide, women encounter
Similar moments of joy,
Shared pain and sufferings
As we tend to those we adore.

It has been our albatross of sorts
To guide and lend a hand,
To strengthen our individual families
Toward the betterment of man.

A feat we all embrace
As we populate the race,
Strongly guided
By our individual faiths.

Yes, sisterhood is more than a bloodline,
It runs deeper than the sea.
It is embedded in the nature
Of the female species.

Time

Time is a harsh master
It controls all that we do,
From the time we are born
Until the time we die,
Never releasing us, until it is through.

We do this at this time
And that at another,
Never finding time
To simply enjoy time!

From the time we arrive
We are fighting against time,
To accomplish a fulfilling life
Never knowing when our time is up
We continue to fight the fight.

Good health, poor finances, true love…
We might never find,
All constructed around this concept
Of the impending lack of time.

Someone once told me
"Time is of the essence"
I never quite knew what that meant!
Time is a valuable commodity,
Never to be uselessly spent.

Yes, time is a harsh master
Never relenting its grasp,
By the time you realize
The value of time
Your time is almost up.

We do what we can with the time we have,
Try to change the world, make a difference somehow.
We try to work it all in
Before the time slips by.

Music

"The sound that soothes the savage beast."

Where are the soulful serenades
The soft, sultry sounds of jazz
The melodic rhythm of beats
That stirs the soul of man?

Have we sated our inspiration?
No more ballads to create
No concertos to compose
No symphonies to orchestrate.

Must we rely on greatness past,
To secure sounds for our future?
Reproduce what once was
In lieu of something original.

The challenge for the next generation
To produce sounds of inspiration
Sounds so unique and grand.
They will soothe the soul of man.

Self

Beside myself…by myself
Inside myself…by myself
Outside myself…by myself
Where in lies myself?

Behind myself in worth
Beyond myself in dreams
Inside myself in thought
Outside myself in deeds
Why try to define myself?

Lost myself in life,
Found myself in love.
Is fear the answer to self?
Is love the answer to self?
Only self can define self!

Money

Good money, bad money
Clean money, dirty money
Or is it all just money?

The deeds we do to acquire it
Determine how we label it.
The paper itself is useless
The value is in the desire,
The willingness to do anything
To amass a small fortune...

It was created as a bartering tool
To enhance the medium of exchange.
We've turned into a "God" of sorts,
Selling our souls for gain.
This thing we call money
Has taken control of our lives.
It now dictates to us
How we will survive.

We might want to create
A better system of trade,
Where money is no longer the guiding force
For the exchanges made...

It would eliminate the overpaid
Help uplift the underpaid

Even out the never paid
Keep us all from being waylaid.
This…thing…called…money!

GREED

The dictionary defines greed as: an excessive desire to acquire or possess more than one needs or deserves, esp. of material wealth.

Why be greedy?
Help the needy!

The world would be a much better place
If we all lived according to need.
To be satisfied with good health
Instead of our obsession with greed.

The world would have us think
That more is always best,
When in truth
More is often less.

To sustain the body
Requires less than would seem.
It's the false advertisements
Which inflate our dreams.

To acquire financial security
Is a blessing beyond measure
To not worry over the necessities of life
Is truly a God-given treasure.

Wouldn't it be nice
To share what we have

With all those in need?
To rise above selfishness,
Put aside greed.

None would suffer in this "perfect world"
All would have what they need.
We'd only have to put aside
Our wanton desires and greed.

Why be greedy?
Help the needy!

Man from Corinth

There once was a man from Corinth,
Whose fortune entirely he'd spent.
He'd inherited from his dad
His dad from his dad
So forth the story went.

Well, one day this man from Corinth,
Whose fortune entirely he'd spent,
Had a desire to rebuild his empire.
Alas, he had not a cent.

So he came up with an idea,
He was excited and full of zeal.
Unfortunately, it had no appeal
To those who would finance his deal.

Now this man from Corinth,
Whose fortune entirely he'd spent,
Would not succumb to defeat…
He revamped his plan, took a new stand
And again decided to compete.

He entered himself into a contest
The winner to be financially blessed.
All he had to do was tell a lie or two
In order to win the coveted cash.

He felt ill at ease
With doing corrupt deeds
But desperately wanted the cash.
He put aside his integrity
To justify his immorality,
Alas, he did not succeed.

So now this man from Corinth
Whose fortune entirely he'd spent
Still did not have a cent.

He recognized his need to repent.
He fell to his knee,
To God he did plea
To end his earthly torment!

He asked for forgiveness
From his deceitfulness,
Determined to live right
In spite of his financial plight.

Thus the man from Corinth
Whose fortune entirely he'd spent,
Recognized the true value of life,
Chose to live godly, and accepted a wife.

The woman he chose said not a word,
Married for love, trusted God above.
A year after their marriage she did confess
To the love of her life, that she was financially blessed.

So now this man from Corinth,
Whose fortune entirely he'd spent,
No longer had concern for a cent
As a result of his new commitment.

Healing

The human body is a miraculous machine,
Its restorative powers amazing.
Our Creator saw to everything,
His design, still being admired.

Study as we might
We cannot unravel the mystery
As to how all the parts interact.
We have a vague idea, but no concrete facts.

We examine with microscopes
Cut up into little pieces
Trying to discover
What God made easy.

This forces us to acknowledge
The limits of our creativity.
We are but mere mortals
Without divinity.

Man continues to emulate God,
Trying to recreate humanity
With his endless flaws.

It is not up to us
To recreate of the master,
But to accept what is done
Before we create disaster.

To be able to care for ourselves is one thing,
Trying to be God is
Blasphemy!

Highs and Lows

So high…thought I could fly
So low…didn't know which way to go
So free…couldn't stand being me
So sad…damn near went mad
But there's always drugs to be had!

Get my party on…
What's my poison of choice?
What will it be?
Can't make up my mind
Will do at least three.

Snort way too much blow
My mind oblivious…no one will know
So numb…can't feel a thing
Heart pounding…can hear my ears ring.

Went too far…must bring myself down
Smoke a little pot…try to unwound.
Drink a little booze…help ease my pain
Get my groove on…why should I abstain?

So high…though I could fly
Went too far…now I die!

Crack and Meth

The enemy comes but to steal, kill, and destroy
His choice against man a mere toy
It's use attractive to both girl and boy.
Once in its grasp, the battle you fight is yours
Mind against body, the Spirit man ignored.

A desire so strong you succumb to degradation,
Wondering when it got this way
It was only supposed to be for play.

Now you'll do anything to fulfill your need
Debase yourself, in order to feed
The monster that's taken over you!

Women sell their bodies, men do too!
Do all sorts of things, they wouldn't normally do.
Lie, cheat, steal, and break the law
Avoid those who love them
Because of their self-imposed flaw.

How do we fix this broken soul?
They have to want to get better, or so I'm told.
It is a disease of the body and the mind
Lost in make-believe, reality hard to find.

We've lost so many to this destructive force.
The enemy is having a field day
Using us against ourselves, of course.

We're making his work easy for him,
Succumbing to temptations of the flesh.
We've got to find a way to rid the world
Of this crack, cocaine, and meth.

The Evil One

Be wary of the evil one,
He is out to seduce your mind.
He'll use every weapon in his arsenal,
Employ every trick he can find.

His desire…to destroy mankind.
His goal, to undermine God.
He's nothing more than an adversary,
An angry, resentful, clod.

His methods are all-consuming,
His resources…a never-ending stream.
His arm is far-reaching,
He'll even invade your dreams.

Fortify your soul against him,
Gird your heart with truth.
Cover your mind with wisdom,
The Word of God he can't break through.

Never underestimate his talents,
He'll use them at every turn.
His objective is very simple,
He wants to see us burn!

To join him in his misery,
Trying to prove God wrong.
A useless battle he's fighting,
Jesus has already won!

So be wary of the evil one,
He does not wish to be alone.
He'll attack, seduce, and undermine,
He'll upend every stone!

LIVING DEATH

We walk…
We talk…
We move…
Aimlessly flowing through life.
Unaware of our own existence,
Constantly fighting the fight.

We are born to die
While striving to reach our full potential.
Struggling to reach goals
Which somehow seem essential.

Never acknowledging our own mortality,
Living lives full of immorality.
Where's the purpose?
What are we here to do?

Give God the praise,
Give God the glory!
Honor him,
For our life's story.

Destruction

Destruction, devastation, death.

People die continuously,
Not all of natural cause.

The mind of man is warped,
His actions taken flawed.

We destroy, devastate, annihilate,
Seemingly void of awe.

Where does the cruelty come from?
Is it an inherent flaw?

Why torture, destroy, violate?
Have we no conscience at all?

Man is de-evolving,
Barely human at all!

Decisions

Homicide
Suicide
Genocide

We're destroying ourselves from within.
No need to fear outsiders,
We'll be the cause of our own end.
How to stop this madness?
Where do we begin?

By taking control of our emotions,
Not allowing them to control us.

By taking back our children,
Teaching them to love then trust.

Returning to the ways of God,
Which have stood the test of time.

Assume responsibility for our actions,
Stop blaming others for our shortcomings.

It's time for us to decide!

FEAR

The spirit of fear…
An immobilizing emotion,
A myriad reasons why.
What causes one to tremble,
May cause another to die.

Ghastly shadows of incidents,
Memories of past pain,
Linger in our subconscious,
Causing fear to remain.

Triggers, sporadic and unknown,
Cause us to react
To what terrifies us most
In a senseless fear attack.

A gripping, paralyzing sensation,
One not easily controlled,
Renders us helpless to the "spirit of fear"
An unruly entity which in us abodes.

Loss

We lost control of education
We lost control of child-rearing
We lost control of control...

Our God-given right, as believers
We should have taken a stand
Then, control would have been maintained...

Onward, Christian soldiers
We should have led the way
Surrendered to the world at large
Allowed them to say...

How we entertain our children
When and where we pray
Instead of taking a stand
We allowed the world to decay...

God has not given us the spirit of fear,
but of love and a sound mind
Are we strong enough Christian soldiers?
To turn the world around...

Enveloped in the full armor of God
Why did we surrender the upper hand?
Thus allowing the nonbelievers
To control the destiny of man...

We will be held accountable
For our lack of standing fast
Choosing instead to keep quiet
Rendering the Word of God an impasse…

His word will not return to him void
Eventually this world will be destroyed!

I Believe

(Disclaimer)
The following beliefs were sent to me via email—the author unknown—however, I thought that they should be recorded in print for future posterity. These beliefs are so germane to society; therefore, I've enclosed them as a part of this anthology.

A birth certificate shows that you we were born!
A death certificate shows that we died!
Pictures show that we lived!

I believe...
That just because two people argue,
It doesn't mean they don't love each other.
And just because they don't argue,
It doesn't mean they do love each other.

I believe...
That we don't have to change friends if
We understand that friends change.

I believe...
That no matter how good a friend is,
They are going to hurt you,
Every once in a while
And you must forgive them for that.

I believe...
That true friendship continues to grow

Even over the longest distance.
Same goes for true love.

I believe…
That you can do something in an instant
That will give you heartache for life.

I believe…
That it's taken me a long time
To become the person I want to be.

I believe…
That you should always leave loved ones with
Loving words
It may be the last time you see them.

I believe…
That you can keep going long after you think
You can't.

I believe…
That we are responsible for what
We do, no matter how we feel.

I believe…
That you either control your attitude
Or it controls you.

I believe…
That heroes are the people
Who do what has to be done
When it needs to be done
Regardless of the consequences.

I believe…
That my best friend and I

Can do anything or nothing
And have the best time.

I believe…
That sometimes the people you expect to kick
You when you are down will be the ones
To help you get back up.

I believe…
That sometimes when I am angry
I have the right to be angry, but that
Doesn't give me the right to be cruel.

I believe…
That maturity has more to do with what types
Of experiences you've had, and
What you've learned from them, and less
To do with how many birthdays you've celebrated.

I believe…
That it isn't always enough,
To be forgiven by others
Sometimes, you have to learn
To forgive yourself.

I believe…
That no matter how bad
Your heart is broken,
The world doesn't stop for your grief.

I believe…
That our background and circumstances
May have influenced who we are, but
We are responsible for who we become.

I believe…
That you shouldn't be
Too eager to find out a secret
It could change your life forever.

I believe…
Two people can look at the exact same thing
And see something totally different.

I believe…
That your life can be changed
In a matter of hours
By people who don't even know you.

I believe…
That even when you think
You have no more to give,
When a friend cries out to you
You will find the strength to help.

I believe…
That credentials on the wall
Do not make you a decent human being.

I believe…
That the people you care about
Most in life
Are taken from you far too soon.

Grande Dame

A true legend has departed
A voice filled with truth, grace, and wisdom
A teacher of the highest regard
Encouraged us to face obstacles against all odds
Words of inspiration sprang free from her mind
Insight and vision, ahead of her time
Feats accomplished inspired mankind
What a legacy to leave behind.

Never had I, the pleasure to meet
Reading her words a sublime treat
I now write because of her
For me my own personal superstar
When I first read
I Know Why the Caged Bird Sings
I felt she was talking directly to me
Now she'll never know how she inspired me.
Rest in peace, you awesome woman of God
Know that you touched the world at large!

REFLECTION

Into the mirror I look, what there do I see?
Three alter egos staring back at me.
The me…that I think I am…
The me…that other people see…
The me…that only, God knows me to be…
Mirror, mirror on the wall…
Which one of me will stand tall?

The me…that I feed the most
That will be the ultimate test
Who will win, spirit or flesh?
Will the foolishness of my flesh, cause me to fall?
Or the strength of my spirit man
Build an insurmountable wall.

I must show myself approved
Study, meditate, and fast
To enable my spirit man to surpass
The lust of the eyes, the desires of the flesh
The pride of life, sin's all-inclusive mesh.

How do I overcome temptations so great?
I must surrender to the Word, allow it to permeate
Personal desire just a beginning
Only the Holy Spirit, can help me win it.

The battle I fight is not mine, it belongs to the Lord.
My submission to him, will determine my all
Mirror, mirror on the wall
The God in me will stand…and never fall.

IRREFUTABLE LOVE

"Ask and it shall be given; knock and it shall be answered."

My Spirit inquired of my Lord, *I want to see you…*
He showed me a sky of blue
A rainbow of many colors
Mountain peaks covered in snow
Multicolored wild flowers in the meadow
And I said, "Thank you, Lord!"

My spirit inquired of my Lord, *I want to feel you…*
He blew me a kiss
Trees swayed in the breeze
Snowflakes fell on my face
A light, refreshing tease
And I said, "Thank you, Lord!"

My spirit inquired of my Lord, *I want to smell you…*
Rain fell from heaven
Fresh morning dew
Orchards in full bloom
Fragrant flowers too.
And I said, "Thank you, Lord!"

My spirit inquired of my Lord, *I want to hear you…*
He gave me the sound of the breaking surf
The midnight melody of crickets
The morning love song of birds
The distinct rumble of thunder
And I said, "Thank you, Lord!"

My Spirit inquired of my Lord, *I want to taste you…*
And his "Word" said,
"O taste and see that the Lord is good
His mercy endures forever."
No greater love exists
The Lord gave his all
How dare we resist.
And again… I said, "Thank you, Lord!"

Visions

Many are called
Few are chosen
To voice the heart of God
His word he sends
That we might live
Through his oracles
This gift he gives.

Haiku's

The world is changing
Morality gone astray
Who helps the children?

New technology
Expanding today's outlook
Where will it all end?

Lord Jesus, help us
The end-time is upon us
What do we do now?

Your Word answers all
We need only look to it
To find the results.

Confusion

Has the Sabbath lost its reverence?
Or have people lost reverence for the Sabbath?

God is the same yesterday, today, and forever more
The world is out of order
The people of God must restore.

The fear of the Lord is the beginning of knowledge,
Yet fools despise wisdom.

How do we convince a world, shrouded in confusion?
That their reality…is full of delusion.

How do we protect them from themselves?
Return them to God
In order to save themselves.

He is the only absolute way
To survive in a world full of decay!

WENCH FOR SALE

I dun giv'm er'thang
What mo' dey won't…?
Us to lae down likes wees ded
Wen enuf gon be enuf?
Lawd Jesus…help me!
I bin told, kan't do dis…kan't do dat
Kan't go here…kan't go thar
What us gon do now?
I d'klar folks kan't seem to make up deys mind.
Massa tell me…nigga gal, kum here
Nigga gal go thar
I ain't sure which wae ta go
I jus stans stil.
Wait ta see what dey won't me ta du
Dens I move.
Massa se… I a upty nigga
Dat why he sell me
I laze 'n' good fo' nuthin'
N' ne how I wait'n fer dis heer life be ov'r
Ain't been nut'in but pain
Be betta wen I git to the otha' side
No moe…do this gal
No moe…do that
I jus' be free
Kan't nobody els own me!

Family Reunion

Faces all around me…
Vaguely familiar they look
People I've never seen before
Who bare me a striking resemblance
Pictures of those who came before
Never did I see
Shared characteristics
Directly pertaining to me
A gesture, a look, a smile
Took me by surprise
I was unprepared to see
Myself in all their eyes!

Glory, Glory, Halleluiah!

Mine eyes have seen the glory
Of the coming of the Lord
There were visions so bizarre
They confound the depths of Sheol
There was lying, cheating, treachery
So much, I did deplore, but
God's truth keeps standing strong!

He is almighty, He is all powerful
He is the alpha and omega
The God we all adore
He is the beginning and the ending
Everlasting, and so much more
God's truth keeps standing strong!

Glory, glory, halleluiah!

Flashbacks, Memories, and Dreams

Obscure images floating in the air, *Flashbacks!*
Demure thoughts passing by, *Memories!*
Subconscious visions dancing in my mind, *Dreams!*

Deception

Limited time
Desires achieved
Faith still required
Do not be deceived!
The world evolving
Technology the new need
Future generations
A brand new breed…
God still in control
Do not be deceived!

Reality, Subconscious, and Heart

Reality deals with the five senses.
Subconscious deals with the unfathomable mind.
Heart deals with limitless possibilities.

Relationship

The basis for all interactions:
Personal
Professional
Religious
Financial
Romantic
Familial
The core of our very existence!

Lost and Found

We seek but never find
That which is pure and divine
True love that's meant to last
Complete acceptance of our past
Who we are truly meant to be
Regardless of what others see.

We seek but never find
Total comprehension of the mind
The brain, an organ so complex
It hides from us
Complete awareness of self.

We seek but never find
Treasure or riches sublime
Glory and power yet to be had
Success unlimited,
For us to grab.

We seek but never find
Complexities of relationships
Intertwined
Realities of histories past
Engulfs us all to be free at last!

Right and Wrong

Why is it?
Easier…to do wrong than right
Easier…to lie than tell the truth
Easier…to spend than save
Is it because…wrong is quicker than right
Lies…more believable than truth
Now…more important than later
Or have we simply switched masters.
?

FRUITS OF THE SPIRIT

The complete calm of *Perfect Peace*
The total rapture of *Joy*
The serene awareness of *Love*
Can all be found in the *"Word."*

If you are seeking and cannot find
You have only to study the book divine
To unravel the mystery
Of truth found in history
The world from its inception
To its final decimation
Has been recorded for all to see
In the book called B-I-B-L-E.
Which was written for you and me!

NIG'GAHS

There are two things in life I cannot abide
The first being Nig'gahs, the other flies
Nig'gahs and flies I do despise!

Don't get it twisted
All Nig'gahs ain't Black
It's any group of people
Without scruples or tact!

Any…body of beings, which lack regard
Only interested in self, not the world at large
It is the small mind that will not see
If it affects you, it will also affect me
The earth is a haven, for all forms of life
We cannot allow Nig'gahs to cause us strife!

Nig'gahs and flies I do despise!

7 Cs

The great *commission* given by God
To love one another against all odds
To show *compassion* to our fellowman
To support and encourage when they need a hand
Our ability to *compel* one another
To lead them toward Christ
Show *concern* for our fellowman, in this life.
We are expected to show *cooperation*
Encourage one another
Through open *communication*
Instead of false accusations and *condemnation!*

IMPERTINENCE

Confusion, perplexity, indecision
Attacking the mind of man
People unaware of their actions
Slowly losing the upper hand.

Judgment clouded
Memory intermittent
We're slipping into darkness
Seemingly indifferent.

Our subconscious mind
Continually being seduced
The adversary proficient
In tactic use.

This deteriorating predicament
Requires immediate attention
Full use of discernment
To rid ourselves of this impertinence.

Superstar

To be where you are
They never inquire…how you got there
They never inquire…at what cost
They only see the superstar
Shining brightly from afar.

The sacrifice, discipline, and effort
You forced yourself to accept
Made way for your burgeoning talent
Which propelled you to your zenith.

The hurt, the pain, the anguish
The separation you had to endure
Is wasted on the observer
Wanting to be where you are.

Never once wavering
In your determination to reach
That pinnacle of success
Your ultimate feat.

To be where you are
Had an exorbitant price
Only those with fortitude
Will ever reach that far!

SECRETS

To be a fly on the wall
To hear hidden…secrets fall
Could possibly…destroy us all
Being a fly on the wall.

To be invisible in a room
Eerie silence like a tomb
Whispered confessions of doom
Snatched from within a mother's womb.

To be on the outside of a listening door
To hear things you've never heard before
Could cause your mind to want to explore
Things best left, to be examined no more.

Secrets are secret for a reason
All things revealed in due season!

The Earth Is the Lord's

Why quibble we, and fight
For what does not belong to us
Why claim we, what was lost
For temporary possession of
The things we acquire in life
Should only be what we need
For all things will be
Left behind indeed.

Why quibble we, and fight
Over things and not love
For love will transcend with us
Into the heavens above
Things of the heart
Memories attained
These are the true treasures
We must try to obtain.

"The earth's is the Lord's
And the fullness thereof."

WE

We prowl and we growl
We snot and we snare
Hoping to make
Our enemy beware.

We hoot and we howl
We holler and we scream
Trying to make believe
It's only a dream.

The tricks of the enemy
Are real for sure
His deception designed
To create a false lure.

To lead us falsely
In the way we should *not* go
To rob us of the reality
Of what we already know.

So we hoot and we howl
We snot and we snare
Making believe we've got not a care.

Tomorrow

Yesterday is gone
No need to look back
Look only to the future
Prepare for the next attack
We can't change yesterday
Only deal with today
Tomorrow is not promised
But prepare anyway!

FRIENDSHIP

We speak with a similar voice
In life we might make a similar choice
We bond on like beliefs
Those we choose to make our friend.

Sometime opposites attract
They go where we dare not
We feed upon their boldness
It excites our fear or lack.

How we choose our friends is interesting
Each one supplies a different need
Fulfilling in us a vacancy
In actions, thoughts, or deeds.

We look for similar attributes
Life experiences shared
A common desire to achieve
Life's successes.

This is how I choose my friends!

HELP

God places people in our lives
From varied associations
Through work, school, neighbors, and church
To assist us in various plights
We never know who it will be
We are never able to foresee
Whom he's placed to assist us
When we encounter life's difficulties
It is very seldom whom we expect
Sometimes it's those which we ourselves neglect
God's reasoning is beyond our intellect
He always has a ram in the bush
For those who call him Father
He already knows the outcome
His vision sees farther
We need only trust and obey
Follow the course laid
Accept the path he's set for us
Surrender without delay.

Grandma's Prayer

Lawd Jesus, hep us!
Peoplez dun loss dae minz
Folks kan't thank no mo'
Daes lazee n shif-les
What us gon do?
Hab mercee, Jesus!

Father

Provider, protector, man of God
The one we turn to when life is hard
He leads, guides, and directs our path
This man we call father.

He is the strong man in our house
Mom is his inspiration and his spouse
The path he's chosen for us to take
Ensures our success in life will be great.

This man we call father
Showers us with his love
He gains his strength
From his Father above.

This man we call father
Never rest until he's sure
Those whom he is responsible for
Are safe, sound, and secure.

That's why we love and honor him
In our own unique way
To express our thanks, and gratitude
Each and every day.

Grandma's Babies

They came into the world so fast
I was unprepared for the impact
The way in which my life would change
My babies having babies
Seemed so strange.

It seemed like only yesterday
I was just a kid myself
With no thought for tomorrow
Just cruising through life.

Then I was a mother
Responsible for another
The years they seemed to fly past
Here was my babies grown at last.

Starting their own families
Those that came from me, my precious seed
Continues to grow the family
The cycle of life proceeds!

I

Intelligent individuals
who face
Irrational ideologies
which allow
Illiberal incumbents
to foster
Illegal immigrants
causing
Insurmountable and irreconcilable
differences
Illuminating independent
Ideas
For we the people!

GIVING

Lovers are givers
"You can *give* without *loving*, but you can't *love* without *giving*."

When first we met, I wanted to know all there was to know
As we grew closer, I only wanted your feelings to show.

I tried to share with you all that I had
That only seemed to make you mad.

The more I gave, the more you took
I felt like a fish dangling on your hook.

I thought we were both in this together
I thought our love would last forever.

Then I realized it was only just me
I was merely a means for you to be.

You never loved and you never gave
What I offered was a way for you to save.

As soon as you could, you would've walked away
Leaving me torn and led astray.

If you could not give to me what I gave to you
Why the pretense at loving me too?

Had you but asked, I would have given to you
For my love was sincere and true.

Your attempt at falseness and deceitful lies
Has caused my heart to be weary but wise.

Lovers give, they hold nothing back
I trust you've learned this altruistic fact!

SUFFERING

Why do the living suffer more than the dead?
Is it the pain, the loss, or just defeat?
We tend to mourn long after they're gone
We must face our mortality all alone
This terrifies some.

The universal common denominator
Which all men face
We must all at some time leave this place
We are born to die, die we must
Return to the dust of Mother Earth
This terrifies some.

For those of us who choose to believe
Death is nothing more, than a welcome reprieve
We go to be with the Lord at last
Free from this flesh body and its past
This exhilarates some.

No more suffering, no more pain
Just the glories of heaven
Which we hope to attain
This exhilarates some!

Home

We've all heard the clichés
Even recognized their merit.

Home is where the heart is
Be it ever so humble, there's no place like home
Just to name a few.

A place of familiarity, comfort, and peace
That's what you'll find at your home retreat.

A place of complete surrender
From all that we do.

A shelter in the time of storm
A safe place to go to
When things go wrong.

Each home is different, no two alike
Dedicated to its residents
Their preference intact.

Yes, home is where the heart is
There's no denying that fact.

Happiness

A psychological phenomenon or a decided attitude
Wherein lies our happiness?
In tangible accomplishments or emotional beliefs
Do we determine our own state of mind?
Or allow circumstances to dictate how we feel
I believe emotions are swayed by our attitude
And I control my attitude!

BLESSINGS

The blessings of the Lord are continual
Every day when you rise
Things happen, you wonder why
You are not seeing them with your spiritual eye.
The blessings remain a mystery to us
God's revelation will come when we trust
Things are seldom what they seem
After the storm, they relegate to dreams
It's always hardest when passing through
Never forget the Lord is with you
All things happen for a reason
A lesson learned, the start of a new season
The trials and tribulation affect us all
It's how we go through them
That strengthens your call
Always remember and never forget
God is love
He's not finished with you yet!

Jesus

Woe to the unbeliever

        Jesus is soon to return

                Will you be ready?

      Praise him in the glory of his holiness

      Dance before the lord with wild abandonment

        Sing unto him a new song!

            Amen!

Inspirational Acronyms

LOVE = Love Overrides Vengeance Eventually

HOPE = Hanging Onto Positive Expectations

SMILE = Special Magic In Loving Everyone

FEAR = False Evidence Appearing Real

BIBLE = Basic Instructions Before Leaving Earth

PUSH = Pray Until Something Happens

BABE = Born Again Believer Eternally

DOG = Depend On God

Thank You, God

How do we begin to voice our thanks?
Are mere words enough?
We shout, dance, and we sing
Trying to show what loving you means.

We pray and try to live holy
Obey the principles of God
Living in this sinful world
Makes it seem so hard.

It is a good thing that God can read our hearts
Know what's in our mind, even our deepest thoughts
Nothing seems sufficient, for all that You gave
The life of your Son, that we might be saved.

Thank you, God, for being God alone!
Thank you for your love, in spite of our flaws!

Natural Beauty

Mountains majestic, peaks pointing skyward
A stunning example of perfect creation.

Spectacular waterfalls, lush green terrain
Visual imagery beyond acclaim.

Sunrise and sunsets, which take your breath away
The artistry of God impossible to duplicate.

Try as we might, all the greats
They do a good job, but only imitate.

No one can touch, the master's flair
Original creations, nothing else can compare.

The sky, the moon, stars that shine at night
Only increase our visual appetite.

Beauty so pure it pierces the heart
God's divine tapestry, the world in itself…art!

Ten Things to Remember

(Author Unknown)

The value of time

The success of perseverance

The pleasure of working

The dignity of simplicity

The worth of character

The power of kindness

The obligation of duty

The influence of example

The wisdom of economy

The virtue of patience

My Sue

Strong, independent, resilient
Determined, steadfast, persistent
That's my Sue.

Jovial, loving, giving
Warm, inviting, enjoyed living
That's my Sue.

Unwavering in the face of adversity
Entrenched in her faith in God
She stood against the test of time
Battling against the odds.

Large in stature, big hands and feet
Stamina and endurance, couldn't be beat
Fair in appearance, a physical treat
That's my Sue.

Witty, vivacious, and flirty
Alluring, energetic, and sometimes downright dirty
That's my Sue.

But most of all, her love was true
She struggled and scratched to make do
We were protected at all costs
She raised us all without a loss.

The absence of her presence
Will linger forever
I'll miss my Sue
My earthly treasure!

Adversity

Situations which arise to challenge us
Obstacles to overcome which encourage us
Failures to face which inspire us
Disappointments to resolve which strengthen us.

The job of adversity is to uplift us
Increase our faith, make us stronger
Never allow adversity to control you!

SERENITY

The peacefulness of quiet.
The calmness of still.
The relaxation of darkness.
The comfort of familiar.

The Unexpected

You look one day and it's gone
Your youth, your health, your turn
You wonder where it went
Your time elapsed…and spent.

Did you accomplish all of your dreams?
Set them aside for tomorrow
Tomorrow came and went
Your time elapsed…and spent.

Did you travel the world and see
Other countries, cultures, or simply be
Just where you are today
Wasting your precious time away.

It goes by far too quickly
We must stop and take notice
Act as opposed to waiting
Before your day, fades away!

Your time elapsed…and spent.

Victorious God

He's a victor
My God's victorious
He is victorious for all time.

Satan, you don't stand a chance
Just passing time
Trying to steal man's mind.

He's a victor
My God's victorious
He is victorious for all time.

He said he would
I knew he could
He's not a man, that he should lie.

'Cause my God's a victor
He is victorious
He is victorious for all time.

Existence

Life is like a leaf, blowing in the wind
Controls our destiny without end
We think that we have control
There's nothing further from the truth
It acts without reason, rhythm, or proof

Life is like a wisp of smoke, billowing in the air
Vanishes like vapor, seemingly without a care
The cosmos plays tricks, things we cannot perceive
To think we're in control is a falsehood indeed

As man, we were given dominion to rule the earth
Concepts beyond our understanding, we gave no worth
Because we cannot see a thing, does not mean it doesn't exist
It merely means we're limited in the use of our full gift

God has made us able, if only we believe
To overcome all obstacles if we do not become deceived

Yes and No

Hurt me… No
Save me… Yes
Leave me… No
Love me… Yes
Stay for me… No
Grow with me… Yes

Know me… Maybe
Be me… Never!

The Past

Let's not, let go, of the entire past
Some of its lesson were meant to last
Technology is the future; indeed
Not if it destroys realities need

Common sense has damn near departed
The future of mankind possibly thwarted
Consideration for one another must return wholehearted

If not, we face possible extinction
The end of existence as we know it
To usher in a new beginning, a world in itself alien

Let's not let go of the entire past
Some of its lessons were meant to last.

Generation X

This piece is written to the "Baby Boomers"
Those born in the '50s, you know who you are

Millennials have no working concept
Of what we went through
Only the benefit of what they can now do

Don't believe the media propaganda
It's only purpose to belittle and slander
You honestly think you are free and equal
Reality is, we are still a downtrodden people

Wake up, people, and recognize the truth
Hidden behind subversion and reproof
We overcame segregation
However, did not achieve equalization

The veil is barely hidden from view
The distaste for others who are not like you
Inside…we are all the same
Outward appearance doesn't change a thing

Black, brown, yellow, or white
God created us all and gave us life.

Survival

The mistakes we make
The chances we take
The wrongs we do
In life as we go through

They either make us or break us
Control us or destroy us
It all depends upon us
Which way we will go, it's hard to know
It is all in this game we call life!

We each respond differently
No two reactions the same
It is the strength within us
Which determines how we endure life's pain

Some will win, some will loose
Some will fail, some will succeed
Our strength comes from within us
The planting of the seed

Plant good seed, for we reap what we sow
In this game called life
You just never know!

POOKIE

A child of the King has been called to glory
Only those who knew her understood her story
What life has in store we never know
Only God determines when we go
Resting in his bosom, there she'll find peace
Those left behind will mourn and weep

Focus on the time had, remember the good not the sad
A spirit so loving, strong, and pure
A smile so heartwarming, it could lift you up
These treasures remain and will always be with us

Rest, Jacinta, this is not goodbye
Just a pause in our togetherness
We'll see you by and by!

Mama Said

The seed donor of my birth
My acquaintance he did seek
Seventeen years hence delivery
Our meeting would be a first

What could prompt him
At this late date
To express interest in my state?

Where has he been
He's no one to me
Why should I go to see him?
Mama said it would be

Mama said he wants to see you
He's had a heart attack
Wants to make amends for his absence
His parental lack

Makes no difference to me
Mama said we would go
I'll pay my respect
Then see him no more

Just because Mama said!

Time

The perception of time is just for us
An hour, a minute, a second
A day, a week, a month
A year, a decade, a century
A way to measure what's happened to us

A way to record our achievements and gains
A way to monitor our growth and pain

The life span of a man, is just a flicker in time
To be used wisely, not undermined
Your presence on Earth should leave its mark
Either good or bad, light or dark

Only future generations will know your output
Based on their world and its outlook.

GRANDPARENTHOOD

We remember the "Perils of Pauline"…well, these are the "Hiccups of Head."

This is a compilation of short stories involving my number three grandson, whom I lovingly call "Head."

I am an old-school grandma and I firmly believe in "Spare the rod, spoil the child," and that "The rod of correction chases away all foolishness"—two of my favorite Bible scriptures.

My Head has challenged me in all of my supposed maturity and wisdom on how to deal correctly with the curious mind of a child. I hope one of these scenarios, while brief yet true, will help some other parent or grandparent in the rearing of their child.

At the penning of this publication, my Head has reached the tender age of twelve, and I am hoping that most of his boyhood adventures have come to a close. I was so afraid he would not reach puberty, but he is turning into quite the gentleman. However, I am sure there will be future episodes in his teenage years ahead, I just hope I am resilient enough to keep up.

My Head, when he was a tiny tot, was one of those children who never met a stranger. He would talk to any and all passersby. He was simply a very loving and outgoing young boy. As with all children, one must set limits. Head was only allowed to go two houses down from the porch in either direction. So he became the neighborhood greeter. If you happened to be walking down the street, on our side of the street, he would accompany you and chat with you while you walked, until he reached his limit, he would then simply turn around and return to the porch to await the next passerby. While most children were running and playing, he was sitting on the steps waiting for people to come by. If by some chance, I could encourage him to ride his big wheel, he would simply ride along with the folks and chat. I spent many an entertaining afternoon sitting on the porch enjoying my grandson and his antics.

On this bright sunny afternoon, the neighborhood children were out back playing. My neighbor has a miniature Dachshund named Midnight. Midnight plays with the neighborhood children all the time and is virtually harmless. Plus, he's only about two inches off the ground. Well, on this particular afternoon, my grands came to the house. They are vaguely familiar with the neighbor's dog; however, on this particular afternoon, my Head decided he wanted an up-close and personal interaction with Midnight. Since the dog is accustomed to playing with the children, he started barking and began to run. My Head got startled and took off running toward the back door at full speed, screaming at the top of his lungs, *"Open the door! Open the door!"* and of course Midnight was right on his heels. It was the funniest thing you ever wanted to see. He was screaming for dear life, and going as fast as his little legs would carry him. Needless to say, I had to calm him down and take him back over so that he could see that Midnight was only playing with him, and eliminate the possibility of the future fear of dogs.

As usual, the grand's were at my house and my Head was playing in the living room with some cars or blocks or something. Anyway, I had to keep telling him to stop playing with them on the coffee table and to put them on the floor. He continued to disobey me and I became exasperated and I yelled at him, "*You are going to make grandma spank your ass!*" This shocked him so, he abruptly stopped what he was doing, turned to me and said, *"Grandmas don't say that…mommies say that."* I was so outdone. I had to take time out and explain to him that grandma was very sorry and she didn't mean to yell or curse. As a rule, I never use profanity, so its use was alarming to my Head. I explained to him, "When you do not do what I ask you, it upsets me, makes me say things I would not normally say." It is amazing how children pay attention and recognize things when they are out of order.

This one particular evening, while we were all at the house sitting around and talking the way families do, I asked Head to do something; I can't even recall now what it was that I wanted him to do. In response, he turned around, pulled down his little pants, and proceeded to *show me his little buttocks*. Well, needless to say, I was flabbergasted. I said not a word. I calmly got up, went upstairs, and got my belt. I came back down, went to my chair, and called him to me. He came unsuspectingly. I politely laid him across my lap, pulled down his little pants, and proceeded to spank his naked bottom. Then I explained to him that the only time grandma expects to see his little narrow behind is when she is bathing it or changing his clothes. I can only surmise that he saw some other child in daycare do it and get away with it. I explained to him that this is unacceptable behavior and that he was never to do it again.

Let's see, how does one be politically correct in telling this type of story? First of all, boys are naturally curious when it comes to the female anatomy, and when they are not used to seeing a thing, when they first encounter it; it is with great curiosity. A girlfriend of mine was visiting from out of town, and needless to say, she is greatly endowed with large breasts. (We are talking 44 triple Ds). Anyway, on this particular evening, she was laying on the floor without her brassiere watching TV, and we were catching up on old times. The grandchildren stopped by to visit; and as Head has never seen breasts that large before, he kept walking past and looking. Finally, he just walked by and *accidently tripped* and fell right on top of my girlfriend and copped him a feel. My girlfriend said, "That little boy just felt me up." I told her never mind, "He was just curious, he has never seen anything that big before." The women in my family are not quite so well endowed. That incident I chalked up to a boy's growing curiosity with the female anatomy.

This is a story about my Head going on a walkabout and taking his younger sister with him to visit an imaginary place called *Pluto Planet*. On this particular evening, after dropping off my two older grandsons at my daughter's house, my Head decided he wants to explore the neighborhood in search of Pluto Planet. It is around six in the evening, and growing dark, everyone was in the house. The two older boys were in the bedroom playing video games. My daughter was in the kitchen frying chicken, thinking the two younger ones were in the living room watching TV. My Head, along with his younger sister, slipped out of the front door to go for a stroll in the neighborhood. The neighbors said they were walking by hand and hand, speaking to people as they passed by; they said it was quite cute. The problem came when they reached the large intersection in the neighborhood and someone spotted them, two young children walking unescorted, and called the police. The police picked them up and asked them where they were going and my Head, being Head, said "To Pluto Planet." The policeman asked them if they knew where they lived and they both said yes and proceeded to showed him how to get to their house. Needless to say, the policeman brought them home and, following protocol, proceeded to arrest my daughter, who had no idea they were even gone, for parental neglect. Social Services was contacted and the children were sent home with me until the next day when they could properly sort this situation out. When the social service agent arrived at my home and questioned my Head, she quickly realized this was nothing more than a child's fancy and there were no charges pressed against my daughter. Meanwhile, how to punish him and make him aware that this type of behavior is unacceptable? It took me three days before I was calm enough to discipline him, and his sister also for blindly following after her brother.

The internet/Facebook is a wonderful invention. As with most young people, my Head has his own Facebook page. He was only allowed to have it if he befriended both his mother and me. Well, one evening, while perusing Facebook, I logged into his page and was surprised to find a picture of him with some type of hand gestures on his page. As I am not up with the current youthful displays, and me being grandma, I did what I thought appropriate. I put a message on his page that read, *Grandma is going to need you to take that down, Grandma does not like it.* Well, apparently, saying "grandma" on his page was not cool. His friends gave him a hard time about my use of "grandma" in my verbiage to him. Psychological warfare is great; it reaches farther than you could possibly imagine. So now, not only is he leery about what he puts on his page but also all of his friends, since they know "grandma" will be watching.

About the Author

First of all, I must state that my Head is leery of bugs. His head is like a swivel stick the whole time he is outside. He is constantly on bug patrol. Well, on this occasion, we were at my uncle's home in Virginia. My uncle lives out in the country. In his yard are all types of jungle gyms and seesaws for the children to play with. He has volleyball nets and the like. Anyway, my Head was outside playing and ran into a spiderweb. He comes running into the house saying he thinks he's swallowed a spider and he thinks his *uvula* is swelling up. I take him into the bathroom and make him wash his face and hands. I let him gargle with peroxide to kill his imaginary germs and keep his *uvula* from swelling. How many twelve-year-olds do you know even know what a *uvula* is, let alone where it is? Only my Head comes up with this stuff. At any rate, the panacea cure from Grandma always works. I pray I will have the fortitude to handle whatever he comes up with during these upcoming teenage years.

Perhaps more adventures will follow.
You will have to stay tuned for my next book.

This book is available for purchase at:

Amazon.com

BarnesandNoble.com

E-BookTime.com

To contact the author, please email:

joymitchellbooker57@gmail.com

CPSIA information can be obtained
at www.ICGtesting.com
Printed in the USA
FSHW021847181021
85461FS